Walther Ziegler

Hegel
in 60 Minutes

Translated by
Alexander Reynolds

My thanks go to Rudolf Aichner for his tireless critical editing; Silke Ruthenberg for the fine graphics; Lydia Pointvogl, Eva Amberger, Christiane Hüttner, and Dr. Martin Engler for their excellent work as manuscript readers and sub-editors; Prof. Guntram Knapp, who first inspired me with enthusiasm for philosophy; and Angela Schumitz, who handled in the most professional manner, as chief editorial reader, the production of both the German and the English editions of this series of books.

My special thanks go to my translator

Dr Alexander Reynolds.

Himself a philosopher, he not only translated the original German text into English with great care and precision but also, in passages where this was required in order to ensure clear understanding, supplemented this text with certain formulations adapted specifically to the needs of English-language readers.

Bibliographic Information held by the German National Library: The details of the original German edition of this publication are held by the German National Library as part of the German National Bibliography; detailed bibliographical data can be found online at www.dnb.de.

© 2016 Dr Walther Ziegler
1st Edition June 2016
Jacket design and graphic design for the whole book: Silke Ruthenberg, making use of illustrations by:
Raphael Bräsecke, Creactive – Studio for Advertising, Comics & Illustrations
© JackF - Fotolia.com (image-frames)
© Valerie Potapova - Fotolia.com (image-frames)
© Svetlana Gryankina - Fotolia.com (speech-balloons)

Publisher and Printing:
BoD – Books on Demand, Norderstedt
ISBN 9783741227677

Contents

Hegel's Great Discovery — 7

Hegel's Central Idea — 24
- Dialectics – The Motor of Thought — 24
- Dialectics and the Idea of *Aufheben* — 28
- The Logic of Becoming — 33
- The Master-Slave Dialectic — 39
- The Dialectical Movement of World History — 54
- The Self-Developing World-Spirit as God — 64
- The Cunning of Reason — 68
- The Final Goal of History — 74

Of What Use is Hegel's Discovery for Us Today? — 87
- Is There Reason in History or Has the "World-Spirit" Failed Us? — 87
- To Think Dialectically is to Think Critically — 92
- To Live Means to Change — 98
- Hegel for Managers — 103
- Using Hegel to Go Beyond Hegel — 106

Bibliographical References — 111

Hegel's Great Discovery

Hegel (1770 – 1831) is one of the most significant philosophers who ever lived. Already on his contemporaries he exerted enormous fascination; intellectuals from all over Europe came to Berlin to hear the famous professor. His lectures were legendary – despite the daunting nature of both his personal appearance and his writing style. His facial features were rough: a downturned mouth and a gaze sombre to the point of being painfully piercing. His language was equally unprepossessing. His writings display an eloquence which, because it persists lengthily in pure abstraction, is often opaque and even impenetrable.

Hegel's sympathizers found this quality admirable; his opponents were angered and outraged by it. Hegel's contemporary Schopenhauer was infuriated by the over-complex style of expression that had come, at this time, into fashion among university philosophers and saw Hegel as the main culprit: "But the height of audacity in serving up pure nonsense, in stringing together senseless and extravagant mazes of words such as had previously been heard only in madhouses, was finally reached in Hegel."[2] The famous American philosopher of culture Will Durant also called Hegel's books "masterpieces of obscurity [...]"[3]

Not everyone, then, was well disposed toward Hegel. The abstractness and ambiguity of his language led to his being interpreted also by his posterity in very different ways. Some saw in him a reactionary "court philosopher" to the autocratic Prussian state; others, by contrast, a visionary social reformer; while still others interpreted him as a great mystic. His work remains the object of such interpretative controversies still today.

But one thing is certain: For all the abstractness of his chosen language, Hegel made a magnificent discovery. He was the first philosopher to recognize all the implications of the notion of "becoming". One might describe him as the Charles Darwin of philosophy.

Because for Hegel everything is in constant motion. Human life has as much the character of a process as do Nature and History. A human being comes into the world as a tiny baby and becomes a child, an adolescent and finally an adult. Likewise, human history marches onward from small beginnings. One epoch follows another. New states arise and laws too are repeatedly adapted to fit the new epoch. Not even justice stands as an unalteringly valid standard but likewise changes with time. What was just for one epoch often counts as unjust for the next. Even truth – i.e. that which people consider to be correct and objectively so – changes in the course of history.

Thus Aristotle, for example, in the age of Classical Greece, held slavery to be quite natural and just. He counted slaves as part of *ta onta*, mere household objects. Today, however, slavery is forbidden and punishable as a deprivation of liberty. From such facts Hegel draws the radical conclusion that even truth is not a timeless ideal but rather a living process.

Everything – literally everything – is in constant motion: people's convictions, morality, justice, law and the bodies of legislation, even art, music and architecture. In seeking truth, Hegel argues, one must avoid taking any phase of development for the absolute truth; rather, one must understand the whole process. This conviction is summed up in one of Hegel's most famous statements:

> The True is the whole. But the whole is nothing other than the essence consummating itself through its own development.[4]

Even English-speaking people today often encounter the German word *Zeitgeist* – meaning "spirit of the age" – in newspapers and books. Most of us are unaware that this is an idea which we owe to Hegel's great discovery that every epoch possesses a specific spirit that completely permeates it. *Geist*, indeed – the part of this composite term which corresponds to "spirit" – is perhaps the key term in Hegel's philosophy. And, as the entry of *Zeitgeist* into our language suggests, it is a term that is impossible to translate entirely adequately into English.

Whereas the English language separates the spiritual and the intellectual aspects of human self-awareness from one another and uses "spirit" to describe the first and "mind" to describe the second, the German language combines both these aspects in the single word *Geist*. In the various English editions of Hegel,

Geist has sometimes been translated as "Spirit" – lending a religious-mystical colouring to Hegel's arguments – and sometimes as "Mind" – lending them rather a rationalist-intellectual colouring. But for Hegel this distinction between the "spirit" of an age and its intellectual "mentality" did not really exist. Therefore, we shall retain the term *Geist*, which evokes both "spirit" and "mind", in what follows.

Hegel's *Geist*, then, changes, in the course of history and constantly takes on new forms. But for certain periods of time the thinking and feeling of an entire epoch is marked by a common spirit. One such *Zeitgeist* was, for example, absolutism, with its single all-powerful monarch at the head of the state. Its equivalent in Europe today would doubtless be the spirit of democratic pluralism. In each respective guiding idea of an epoch – or, as Hegel says, in its "guiding principle" – there is reflected the self-understanding and self-awareness of its people. The *Weltgeist* – once again, a term that we need to understand as meaning both "World-*Mind*" and "World-*Spirit*" – elaborates the inherent principle of each historical stage into a multitude of typical trends and phenomena. For example: aristocrats in the Age of Absolutism wore, all over Europe, similar wigs and corsages, listened to the same works by Vivaldi, Handel and Mozart when they went to the opera, and built their castles in the same Baroque style with halls of mirrors, French-style gardens and fountains. This is why Hegel can say:

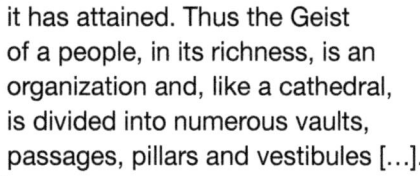

Geist, in each case, has elaborated and expanded in the whole domain of its manifold nature the principle of the particular stage of self-consciousness to which it has attained. Thus the Geist of a people, in its richness, is an organization and, like a cathedral, is divided into numerous vaults, passages, pillars and vestibules [...].⁵

The *Zeitgeist*, says Hegel, is so extremely rich a thing because it embraces not just the current fashion in clothes or furniture but extends also to the music, painting, architecture, state constitutions and even the philosophy of the age concerned. Hegel speaks, therefore, of how any "snapshot" image of a particular age will tend to capture one of the many individual forms of *Geist* that mankind has brought forth in the course of history:

Hegel's Great Discovery

Each (moment) is itself [...] a complete individual shape.[6]

The form of *Geist* manifest in the Romanesque era, for example, is a different form from that manifest in the Gothic or Baroque era; and the form of *Geist* that we see in the Age of Absolutism is different from that which we see in the Age of Enlightenment. When we see temples, statues or paintings from past eras, we can usually easily assign them to a specific period. We do not have to be art-historians to recognize that the Acropolis with its marble columns belongs to the form of human *Geist* manifest in Classical Antiquity or a crusader's castle to that manifest in Medieval Christian feudalism.

Thus far, Hegel's discovery of the dimension of "becoming" appears a simple, uncontroversial thing. For who would contest that history has indeed displayed such "spirits of the ages", i.e. different forms of collective *Geist* pervading different epochs?

But in fact Hegel contends more than this. He also

made a second discovery of great consequence. The various forms of *Geist*, he claims, do not succeed one another by chance or arbitrary choice but rather according to a logical principle of motion: the so-called "dialectic". Hegel initially compares the logical sequence of forms of *Geist* in history with the growth of a plant. Because the phases of a plant's growth and maturation are not just blind and senseless changes but rather follow an inner principle and have a definite goal, even if this goal is not immediately recognizable:

> The plant [...] does not lose itself in mere indefinite change. From the germ much is produced when at first nothing was to be seen. But the whole of what is brought forth, if not developed, is yet hidden and ideally contained within itself. But this coming without itself has an end in view. Its completion fully reached, and its previously determined end, is the fruit [...].[7]

Just as the plant is first a seed and a germinating bud, which then brings forth leaves and flowers, before finally bearing its fruit, human history too follows an inner logic. Each form proceeds logically from the form that preceded it. This is what Hegel calls "dialectics".

Hegel's dialectic, indeed, is not just a matter of growth and harmonious development of latent forces but rather proceeds by way of crises and contradictions.

Hegel portrays the transition from one phase of life into another as often dramatic. Just as a child, on reaching puberty, suddenly no longer wants to be a child subject to others' tutelage and begins violently to question and reject all that adults tell him, so too are epochal transitions in world history characterized by crises, conflicts and contradictions. Hegel often used this term "contradiction" in his works. He meant by it a sense (felt either by an individual or by a whole people) that two things or notions are incompatible with one another.

Hegel saw nothing bad in "contradiction" in this sense; on the contrary, he saw it as something highly beneficial:

> It is only in so far as something has a contradiction within it that it moves, is possessed of instinct and activity.[8]

When, for example, an historical period contains "contradictions" in this sense – i.e. when many people are dissatisfied with the state of society and their own condition in it – revolt arises both in the mental and the material sphere. The old order is toppled and replaced by a new one. Let us take the example of the French Revolution and the transition from absolutism to enlightenment.

Out of resistance to the aristocracy, the doctrine of "divine right", feudalism and serfdom there gradually arose a new form of *Geist*: that of rationalism and enlightenment. The mystically religious notions of the king's rule being ordained by God, and of the aristocracy's having some special "blue blood", gave way to the rational idea of popular rule and human equality.

Hegel was deeply impressed, above all in his youth, by the radical ideas of the French Revolution. He felt that motion had been reintroduced into European history by the "contradiction" raised by the French thinkers of the "Century of Enlightenment" (the 18th Century) and the revolutionaries inspired by them:

> The political condition of France at that time presents nothing but a confused mass of privileges altogether contravening thought and reason [...] an empire characterized by destitution of right [...]. The new Geist began to agitate men's minds [...]. The change was necessarily violent because the work of transformation was not undertaken by the government [...]. The conception, the Idea of right asserted its authority *all at once* and the old framework of injustice could offer no resistance to its onslaught [...]. This was, accordingly, a glorious mental dawn.[9]

It is as a "glorious mental dawn", then, that Hegel celebrates the dialectical upheaval. But it is not just the great revolutions but also many smaller contradictions and upheavals that carry mankind, each time, a little way onward. Hegel sees each new form of *Geist* succeeding and relieving its predecessor by driving itself, in pursuance of dialectical reason, beyond this predecessor's self-established limit. In the exalted and passionate style that he often adopted, Hegel speaks of an "imperial" succession, in human history, of forms of *Geist*:

> The realm of Spirits (Geister) which is formed in this way in the outer world [...] constitutes a succession in Time in which one Geist relieved another of its charge and each took over the empire of the world from its predecessor.[10]

Geist drives itself onward propelled by its own contradictions. The movement begins with a "thesis" – that is to say, the initial leading idea; then comes a contradiction of this idea, or what Hegel calls an "antithesis"; and finally a "synthesis", a new form of

Geist which both abolishes and preserves the preceding "thetic" and "antithetic" forms. In time, however, this "synthesis" itself becomes a "thesis" forming the starting point for a new dialectical upheaval.

The "hard" sciences too, argued Hegel, live and grow by this movement of thesis, antithesis and synthesis. For centuries people believed that the earth was a disc over which the stars were arranged in the sky; sailors were even afraid of falling off its edges. Then certain scientists contradicted this and claimed the earth was round. Eventually a "synthesis" of these two positions emerged in the form of the doctrine that the earth, although indeed round, was the round central point of all the universe, around which the stars were indeed arranged as bodies circling this round central point. This synthesis persisted for many more centuries until it was pushed into the role of a "thesis" to the "antithesis" of Copernicus, who contradicted it by claiming that the earth was really located only at the rim of the universe and itself circled another heavenly body, the sun. We owe, in short, not just our present understanding of our place in the universe but all our reason and all the knowledge we possess regarding ourselves and our world to that work of thesis, antithesis and synthesis that was performed by our predecessors:

> This possession of self-conscious reason which belongs to us of the present world (is) [...] an inheritance and the *result* of labour – the labour of all past generations of men [...].[11]

But Hegel did not dare just to formulate, with his dialectic of thesis, antithesis and synthesis, a law of motion for the sciences, for Nature and for global history. He went still further and applied his great discovery of the centrality of "becoming" even to God Himself.

Not even God, argues Hegel, was there from all eternity. He did not precede the world and simply decide one day to call it into existence. On the contrary, it was only in and through the long labour of the world's history that God was able to bring Himself forth as God. God, then, on Hegel's understanding of Him, is an entity constantly "in progress" and thereby constantly in motion. Hegel prefers, indeed, to speak not of God but of the *Weltgeist* – a term, as we have said, that needs to be understood both as "World-*Mind*" and as "World-*Spirit*" – in order to better bring to expression this aspect of constant "becoming". What Hegel calls the *Weltgeist*, then, is simply the sum total of the various individual "forms of *Geist*", or individual epochs, that mankind has passed through in its history and continues to pass through today:

For (universal) history is the exhibition of the divine, absolute development of Geist in its highest forms – that gradation by which it attains its truth and consciousness of itself.[12]

For Hegel, then, there is no timeless eternal "divinity" hovering over all. The divinity is rather in the midst of life and constantly in motion. The Hegelian *Weltgeist* unfolds itself, out of the simplest and most primitive beginnings, in and through the individual human beings who make up world history and only thereby achieves its "consciousness of itself":

> But the Weltgeist does not sink into this rest of indifference [...] for its activity is its life.[13]

The passionately developed central idea of Hegel's philosophy, then – which presents a hundred different faces while remaining, in essence, the same – consists in the conviction that the divine *Weltgeist*, the thinking human individual, and the history of the world are only three different perspectives on one and the same movement: only three distinct ways of looking at one and the same process of Reason's dialectical self-unfolding.

Hegel considers us all to be bound into a gigantic developmental dynamic which draws everything under its spell. In the process of its "coming to consciousness of itself" the *Weltgeist* grows in and through the succeeding generations of human beings, inasmuch as we drive the development of this "World-Spirit" on through that human thinking and acting that constitutes the world's history. Man becomes more and more like God as his consciousness and his knowledge grow more and more refined in the course of this history.

This new and radical worldview of Hegel's, whereby the dialectical self-movement of Reason occurs at the same time under the forms of God, Man and History, raises, of course, a whole series of questions. Firstly, in what exactly does this motivating dialectical principle which maintains everything in motion consist and how, concretely, does it function? Secondly, is it the divine "World-Spirit" or is it Man himself who determines the course of history? Are we mere marionettes of this "World-Spirit" or is it we who are the true actors in history? And thirdly, where does history end? Is it really possible for Man, in the end, to become God?

Hegel's Central Idea

Dialectics – The Motor of Thought

For Hegel, what he calls "dialectics" is the true motor of all developments occurring in the world. Like a torrent it carries everything with it: the individual consciousnesses of human beings; the events that mark epochal changes in whole societies; and even Nature itself. Everything follows this same dynamic of thesis, antithesis and synthesis.

In the case of the individual consciousness this goes as follows: first, one forms an opinion; then a contrary opinion; until finally a third stance takes form which proves to be free of contradiction. But eventually even this initially non-contradictory synthesis which emerges as a third step takes on the role of a thesis to another antithesis and the process of thought begins anew.

In Hegel's view the individual has no choice but to think dialectically. Ever since the Stone Age, Man's learning has proceeded via errors and contradictions; it is only in this way that the species has acquired the experiences necessary for its survival. If a Stone Age man ate a poisonous toadstool and found himself crippled with stomach pains, both he and those who observed him in this state had necessarily to draw the conclusion not to eat mushrooms – or at least to eat them only in very small quantities until they were able to distinguish the poisonous from the non-poisonous types. The "thesis", then, in this case would run: "mushrooms taste good and satisfy hunger". The "antithesis" would run: "mushrooms are poisonous and must on no account be eaten". And finally, the resulting "synthesis": "It is possible to distinguish edible from poisonous mushrooms and, choosing carefully, enjoy the edible ones." Likewise in all other areas of life, says Hegel, we need to constantly renew our knowledge, so that our lives are indeed a long dialectical process of negating ideas while at the same time preserving them in a higher form.

Our reason, then, operates constantly in this dialectical "three-step" form. Whether it is a matter of the more or less painful eventualities of daily life, great scientific steps forward, or general personal learning-processes, dialectics always plays a role. The result, moreover, of such a dialectical process of thought need not be anything purely theoretical. All that we call experience is in fact acquired dialectically in Hegel's sense:

> Inasmuch as the new true object issues from it, this *dialectical* movement which consciousness exercises on itself and which affects both its knowledge and its object, is precisely what is called *experience*.[14]

In the light of the toadstool example Hegel's meaning here is clear. Hegel says that the dialectical movement is also called experience. This is so inasmuch as the synthesis which emerges from the process of knowledge represents, however painful the eating of the poisonous mushrooms may have been, indeed a valuable experience which benefits future nutritional behaviour. In this light it is also clear what Hegel means when he says that the dialectical movement is one "which consciousness exercises on itself" so that this movement "affects both its knowledge and its object" to such a point that a "new true object issues from it". The "object", in our example, is the (poisonous) mushroom. The man who eats it, being hungry, initially "knows" the mushroom as nourishment which will sate his hunger and "knows" himself as someone in search of such nourishment. After the painful experience that the "object" here – i.e. the mushroom – is not nourishing but rather poisonous, the man finds not just his knowledge of the "object" altered but also his knowledge of himself. He no longer thinks of or defines himself as a being capable of digesting any and every mushroom, just as he no longer thinks of or defines mushrooms as edible objects, now thinking of them cautiously and provisionally as generally dangerous and potentially poisonous.

But this new "antithesis", or new "truth" regarding both himself and the object of his knowledge, is "set in motion" once again when he himself, or others, establish, after careful tasting of small quantities, that not all mushrooms cause nausea and stomach cramps, but only a few. In this way, in Hegel's phrase, there "issues forth for consciousness" yet a third (provisional) truth regarding both mushrooms and the awareness of mushroom-eaters: namely, that not the whole class of such plants, but only certain definable instances thereof, are poisonous and unfit for human consumption.

Dialectics and the Idea of Aufheben

Some pages back, in our general description of Hegel's great discovery, we met with a German word – *Geist* – which we described as both key to Hegel's philosophy and untranslatable into English. In order to fully explain Hegel's notion of "dialectics" we need to look at another such word: *aufheben*.

Like *Geist*, *aufheben* is a word that is philosophically useful to Hegel because it combines ideas that may at first seem unconnected, and even unconnectable, with each other. The word itself, one might say, is a kind of compressed philosophical argument. But this is not to say that it is a technical term understood only by philosophers. *Aufheben* is a word that is used daily, in many simple practical contexts, by German-speakers still today. Most, however, probably do not notice that they use this word in three senses that are quite distinct and even contradictory. Now, it is just this feature of the everyday German term *aufheben* that makes it the ideal term for Hegel to use in his explanations of his philosophy of "progress through contradiction".

One everyday sense in which Germans use *aufheben* is the merely negative sense of "putting an end to" or "removing". This sense certainly applies to the three-term process Hegel describes. On one level, the contradiction between "thesis" and "antithesis" is simply "removed" in and by the "synthesis". Thus "I cannot eat mushrooms" as a contradiction of "I can eat mushrooms" is removed by the "synthetic" stance of "I can eat some mushrooms but not others". Put another way, the contradiction between the initial assumption of mushrooms' general edibility and the second assumption of their general inedibility simply vanishes when the insight is achieved that some mushrooms are edible but others are not.

But, to the puzzlement of the non-German-speaker, Germans can also be heard every day using *aufheben* in the very opposite to this: the sense of "saving" or "preserving". Hegel explicitly refers to this odd feature of the German language in his lectures on logic:

> The word '*aufheben*' [...] has a twofold meaning in our language; it equally means 'to keep', '*to preserve*', and 'to cause to cease', '*to put an end to*'.[15]

This double meaning, of course, serves Hegel's philosophical purpose perfectly. Because, in the "dialectical" philosophical vision he develops, the knowledge achieved through "thesis" and "antithesis" is decidedly not just "put an end to", or "removed", in and by the "synthesis" but rather, on the contrary, carefully preserved as well:

> That which is '*aufgehoben*' (the past participle form of *aufheben*) is thus something at the same time preserved: something that has lost its immediacy but has not come to nothing for that.[16]

Even if the experience of stomach cramps and nausea ceases after some years, when the capacity has been acquired to distinguish healthy from unhealthy mushrooms, to be of any direct significance, this experience is not completely forgotten. It is preserved in the form of the knowledge which anyone who goes looking for mushrooms in the woods now applies. The experience of the dangerousness of certain plants belonging to the class of fungi persists in the care with which the inedible mushrooms are now avoided, along with the experience of the fine taste of the edible ones.

The third – and most literal – sense in which German-speakers use the word *aufheben* is that of "raising" (*heben*) "up" (*auf*). This third sense is clearly also essential to Hegel's idea of "dialectics" because the "synthesis" certainly "raises up" knowledge onto a higher level of consciousness vis-à-vis "thesis" and "antithesis". The knowledge represented by the "synthesis" has, in a certain respect, a higher truth, inasmuch as a differentiated knowledge of the discriminability of fungi from one another in terms of edibility is a knowledge of much greater value and rank than either the first assumption that they were all edible or the second that they were all inedible. This dialectical process of the *Aufhebung* of human knowledge in all these three senses – "removing", "preserving", and "raising up onto a higher plane" – ensures that reason steadily increases its share in this knowledge. People and whole societies acquire experience in just this way, through dialectics pursuing its course within the individual, global history, and Nature. The philosophical system that Hegel established can thus be understood as the ambitious attempt to comprehend the whole of reality as the process of the self-unfolding of just such a dialectical principle of Reason: a Reason, that is to say, which follows its own experiences and drives itself onward by the motor of its own contradictions:

[…] Contradiction […] is the root of all movement and life; it is only in so far as something has a contradiction within it that it moves, is possessed of instinct and activity.[17]

Hegel believed that traditional logic had made a serious error in underestimating the force of contradiction.

The Logic of Becoming

Foundational to classical philosophical logic is the law of identity: A = A. But this law, argues Hegel, leads to a dead, schematic way of thinking which pays attention only to whether an object does or does not accord with the category ascribed to it. If A = A applies, this must logically mean that there cannot, at the same time, apply A ≠ A. Hegel, of course, concurs that such is the case. But he also demands that this line of reasoning be decisively modified. If A = A, then it cannot, he admits, be the case that A ≠ A as well. But it still might well *become* the case that A ≠ A. And for Hegel what counts is indeed *becoming*.

Water, for example, is liquid. But if changes in temperature occur at some point, it can become solid or gaseous. Thus, our knowledge that A = A – in this specific case that 'water = liquid' – can, in living experience, become A ≠ A, so that there grows, out of contradiction, a new knowledge.

This is why Hegel insistently urges us, in his book *The Science of Logic*, to free ourselves, at least to a certain degree, from the static thinking typical of traditional logic, with its "law of identity", and to recognize that it is rather contradiction that is the more important element:

> It is, however, one of the basic prejudices of previous logic and of ordinary thought that contradiction is not as essential and immanent a determination as identity.[18]

Assuming one wants to set up such an artificial hierarchy at all, one should, claims Hegel, rank contradiction as a more profound and essential determination than identity, because it is really only contradiction that brings life and movement into human thinking:

> [...] In fact, if order of precedence were an issue, and the two determinations were to be

> held separate, it would be the principle of contradiction that should be taken as the more profound and the more essential. For [...] identity is only the determination of simple immediacy, of inert being; whereas contradiction is the root of all movement and life [...].[19]

The determination of an object in terms of the law of identity – i.e. 'A = A' – thus achieves no more than the abstract, lifeless registration of a thing's conforming, or failing to conform, to a category.

Hegel, by contrast, emphasizes again and again that negation – i.e. a non-identity, or contradiction – leads thought much further than this. This is so because a contradiction is more than just an abstract non-conformity to a category; a contradiction is always a contradiction with specific traits and qualities; and for contradiction to be concrete and determinate in this way means that the thesis that is contradicted is not simply cancelled out in its entirety; rather, it is recognized as partially false in such a way that its partial falsity (and partial truth) forms a starting point for the further progress of science:

> The one thing needed to *achieve scientific progress* [...] is the recognition of the logical principle that [...] what is self-contradictory does not resolve itself into a nullity, into abstract nothingness, but essentially only into the negation of its *particular* content [...].[20]

If, for example, I have the contradiction that I have eaten one specific mushroom which proved edible, after having eaten many others which proved poisonous, the experience of the edible mushroom is no abstract (i.e. general or indeterminate) cancelling-out of my initial experience that mushrooms can be inedible. It is rather what Hegel calls a determinate cancelling-out of this initial experience – i.e. an opposing to it of the new specific experience that this particular mushroom proved edible. The result of this – to use Hegel's own phrase – "determinate negation" is, then, a higher and more concrete knowledge of mushrooms. Or, as Hegel says:

Because the result, the negation, is a *determinate* negation, it has a *content*. It is a new concept, but one higher and richer than the preceding [...].[21]

It is this "determinate negation", then – or concrete contradiction – that ensures that our world has a dimension of "becoming". Hegel sees the thinking movement of the human mind – and thereby the unfolding of Reason itself – as a drunkenly ecstatic lurching from side to side, from one perspective to its opposite, from thesis to antithesis, wherein neither of these two "members of the process of thought" escapes being drawn along in the dialectical slipstream:

> The True is thus the Bacchanalian revel in which no member is not drunk [...].[22]

But despite the drunkenness of all its members it need never be feared that the thinking process will lose its balance or stumble. Because the tension between those joyfully lurching limbs that are thesis and antithesis, which seem initially to be flying off uncontrollably in different directions, is straight away resolved by the synthesis that advenes in every step. Thus, these two limbs, while being able to draw, as they must, on the two extreme poles of truth, serve in the end, thanks to this synthetic resolution, the simple and placid onward motion of thought:

> The True is thus the Bacchanalian revel in which no member is not drunk. Yet because each member collapses as soon as he drops out, the revel is just as much transparent and simple repose.[23]

What a wonderful image Hegel creates here in order to explain to us thought's dialectical motion. He compares Truth with Bacchus, the ancient god of wine and drunken ecstasy, who lurches along in joyful inebriation but goes his way no less calmly and peacefully for that. It may be worth noting here that Hegel himself, in his student years, was often reprimanded for his excessive fondness for wine consumed over games of cards.

Human consciousness, then, expands its knowledge by way of a Bacchanalian revel of ever more theses, antitheses and syntheses. But it is not just individual consciousness that is driven onward in this way by its contradictions. History too follows this dialectical course, as Hegel shows us by the example of his famous "master-slave dialectic".

The Master-Slave Dialectic

In his best-known and perhaps most influential work, *The Phenomenology of Spirit,* Hegel describes the development of consciousness from its origins up to today. Hegel here compels his readers, over the space of six hundred pages, to re-experience step by step the development of human thought from its first beginnings up to Absolute Knowing, presenting in their turn the many epochs and 'forms of *Geist*' and showing how one emerged from the other. Already in the preface to this book he speaks to his readers of the enormous patience and stamina that he must ask of them:

Since [...] the World-Spirit itself has had the patience to pass through these shapes over the long passage of time and to take upon itself the enormous labour of world history [...] since it could not have attained consciousness of itself by any lesser effort, the individual certainly cannot, by the nature of the case, comprehend his own substance more easily.[24]

In the first chapter of *The Phenomenology of Spirit* Hegel describes the transition from animal perception to human. At this point, there is not yet anything that really corresponds to the *Phenomenology*'s key notion of "self-consciousness" – which, it should be noted, has nothing to do with being "self-conscious" in the sense in which we use this term in normal everyday speech ("I felt self-conscious") but means simply "being aware of being a living, thinking self". At this point, where "self-consciousness" in this strong sense will later arise, there is only what Hegel calls animal "sense-certainty". Life, argues Hegel, is essentially desire. Initially, the desire of consciousness is directed toward mere material objects, such as food. An animal stays permanently on this primitive level of consciousness. It acquires, indeed, through the desire it expresses by eating and digesting food, a sort of "sense of itself". But this "sense of itself" is not yet "self-consciousness" in Hegel's strong philosophical sense.

Self-consciousness in this sense arises only when the desire of a living being comes to be directed no longer toward objects but toward the desire of some other living being than itself. Thus, the essence of love, for example, consists in the fact that desire is no longer directed toward the body of the beloved as a material object but rather toward this beloved's own desire. The man who desires a woman finds his satisfaction not only in her beautiful body but above all in the fact that she, in her turn, desires him too. This means that what the lover seeks is to be loved by his "other". That the feeling of love is so exalting a feeling stems from the fact that the loving gaze of another "self-consciousness" (in this strong philosophical sense) is an especially unconditional way for my own "self-consciousness" to feel itself confirmed as such. As Hegel writes:

> Self-consciousness achieves its satisfaction only in another self-consciousness.[25]

This phenomenon of self-consciousness's feeling itself confirmed and satisfied only in and through another self-consciousness is found, of course, not only in love-relations but in all instances of human beings recognizing and acknowledging other human beings. It is only in the image that others form of our actions, and in their reactions to them, that we recognize who we truly are. By arguing this, Hegel alludes not only to the effects produced by praise or blame in a child – who can feel good or bad about himself depending on whether he is praised or reprimanded – but also to the many forms of recognition and acknowledgment that adults give to each other in daily life. Man is different from the animals not only because he has self-consciosness in this strong sense but also because this self-consciousness is something he acquires only through being recognized by others. When two people meet, the being of each is reflected back to him or to her through the other consciousness's perception; it is the opinion formed of us by the "other" that imparts to each of us what we are:

Each [consciousness] is for the other the middle term through which each mediates itself with itself and unites with itself [...].[26]

But even after human self-consciousness had awoken in this way, the dialectical movement did not come to rest. Already in the moment of its emergence, self-consciousness found itself caught in a contradiction. On the one hand it desired recognition by another self-consciousness. But on the other hand it did not

43

occupy the position in society that would have been required to gain this recognition. There originally existed great inequality between people which consciousness had to overcome. Hegel illustrates this with his famous "master-slave dialectic".

The self-consciousness of the "master" – of the Roman citizen, for instance, or the medieval nobleman – was a greater self-consciousness than that of the slave or serf with whom he shared a world. The master felt himself to be, in Hegel's own words, "the independent and essential consciousness" vis-à-vis the slave and the slave, in his turn, to be a merely dependent and inessential consciousness vis-à-vis the master. Indeed, although the slave, for his part, was forced to fully recognize the master as an independent consciousness, this recognition did not give even to the master what he needed, precisely because it was forced, and arose only from fear of the master's anger. As Hegel writes:

> The outcome is a recognition that is one-sided and unequal.[27]

Since, however, both felt a need to be recognized, both experienced this inequality as a contradiction. At this point Hegel brilliantly explains how this contradiction of unequal recognition is dialectically resolved for consciousness. At first, as we have said, the slave feels dependent and inessential vis-à-vis the independent and essential master, whose orders he carries out:

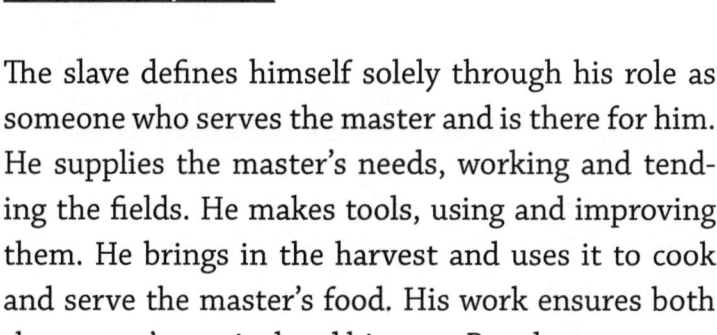

To begin with, servitude has the master for its essential reality, hence the truth for it is the *independent consciousness that is for itself*.[28]

The slave defines himself solely through his role as someone who serves the master and is there for him. He supplies the master's needs, working and tending the fields. He makes tools, using and improving them. He brings in the harvest and uses it to cook and serve the master's food. His work ensures both the master's survival and his own. But the ever greater skill that he acquires thereby strengthens his own self-consciousness. As Hegel writes:

Through work (he) becomes conscious of what he truly is.[29]

This happens because the slave's daily work involves making things, so that he constantly sees the product of his labour before him. By working, forming and fashioning objects, says Hegel, consciousness "makes external" to itself a shape that it has conceived in thought, moulding the objects to fit it. In this way, consciousness recognizes itself as consciousness in these formed objects:

The shape does not become something other than (the slave's own consciousness) through being made external to him; for it is precisely this shape that is his pure being-for-self

> which, in this externality, is seen by him to be the truth. Through this rediscovery of himself by himself (the slave) realizes that it is precisely in his work, wherein he seemed to have only an alienated existence, that he acquires a mind of his own.[30]

It is precisely through labour ordered by someone else, then, that the slave acquires consciousness of being a self. Even if this labour, initially, is imposed on him by the master as something that has meaning only for this master, the slave is able, in the end, to find in it a meaning of his own. When he has, for example, made a new field farmable – removing trees and stones, turning the soil, and watching the corn grow up on it – he is fully aware of what he has done. His work pleases him and he recognizes himself in it, as does the saddler in his artfully fashioned saddle, the coach-builder in his well-built coach, or the smith in a well-forged sword. Thus:

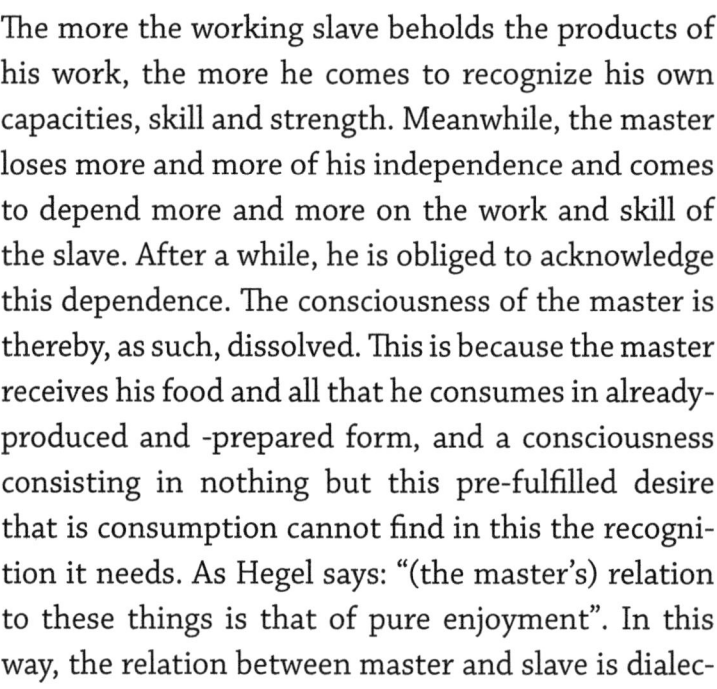

It is in this way, therefore, that consciousness, qua worker, comes to see in the independent being [of the object] its own independence.³¹

The more the working slave beholds the products of his work, the more he comes to recognize his own capacities, skill and strength. Meanwhile, the master loses more and more of his independence and comes to depend more and more on the work and skill of the slave. After a while, he is obliged to acknowledge this dependence. The consciousness of the master is thereby, as such, dissolved. This is because the master receives his food and all that he consumes in already-produced and -prepared form, and a consciousness consisting in nothing but this pre-fulfilled desire that is consumption cannot find in this the recognition it needs. As Hegel says: "(the master's) relation to these things is that of pure enjoyment". In this way, the relation between master and slave is dialectically reversed. It is now the master who is "inessential" and the slave "essential". The only way forward, then, lies in the replacement of the earlier one-sided recognition by a reciprocal recognition:

They recognize themselves as *mutually recognizing* one another.[32]

This chapter of *The Phenomenology of Spirit* is surely one of the richest in historical consequences ever written by a philosopher. It inspired Marx and Engels to develop their materialist dialectic of class struggle whereby the ruling (or "master") class tends historically to produce "its own gravediggers".

It was Marx's and Engels' argument that a whole

series of different forms of "master-slave" relations – slave society proper, of course, but also feudal and bourgeois societies in their turn – had been historically superceded each by the next, with dialectical necessity, due to their respective internal material contradictions.

For example, the "master" class of feudal society, the aristocracy, had, while retaining all political power, been prevented by its traditional concept of honour from engaging in trade or manufacture. It set the peasantry and urban middle class to work for it in these fields and lived off the taxes they paid. But in this way the feudal aristocracy generated a new and confident social class whom Marx and Engels called the "bourgeoisie". This class grew more and more skilled, wealthy and successful until it finally replaced the aristocracy as the political "master" of society. The bourgeoisie, however, even as it "negated" the aristocracy, was creating a new oppressed class, the so-called "proletariat". Marx believed that this class was about to become, in his phrase, "the negation of the negation" and replace, as master of society, the bourgeoisie. It was only, he believed, through a communist revolution that would abolish private property that social contradictions, and thereby history as we have known it, would come to an end.

This interpretation of Hegel's dialectics in Marx's own sense was certainly of historical consequence. A hundred years later, a third of all mankind was living in states that had emerged from such communist revolutions. But Marx had in fact turned Hegel upside down – or rather, as Marx himself preferred to put it, "turned him the right way up again". He turned Hegel's philosophy of mind and spirit into a philosophy of material reality. Although Marx and Engels construe the transformation of the "enslaved" consciousness into a self-determined one in terms of class struggle, this transformation as Hegel conceives of it must be understood primarily as a logical – i.e. mental and spiritual – process.

This chapter about "the master and the slave" and the unfolding of self-consciousness through their dialectic is in fact usually interpreted as describing mankind's acquisition of a modern, "enlightened" mentality, in which the individual's consciousness comes to identify with the consciousnesses of those around him. Human self-consciousness, argues Hegel, learns at the end of its process of development that, if it aspires to live in complete freedom and independence, it is only in unity with other self-consciousnesses – as an "I" that is a "we" and as a "we" that is an "I" – that it can do this:

> What still lies ahead for consciousness is the experience of what Geist is – this absolute substance which is the unity of the different independent self-consciousnesses which, in their opposition, enjoy perfect freedom and independence: "I" that is "we" and "we" that is "I".³³

This sentence occurring at the end of the "master and slave" chapter – whereby human consciousness learns, at a certain point, that *Geist*, although it is an absolute substance that draws its being from the contrast and conflict of the various individual self-consciousnesses, nonetheless creates thereby a unity of all these self-consciousnesses – may seem to be a very difficult one. But the experience it expresses is in fact very simple. It is the experience gained by any individual who lives in a well-functioning society or state: namely, that the "collective spirit" of such a society or state forms the comprehensive unity of all the individuals in it, and that this "collective spirit" succeeds in reconciling with one another all the conflicts that may divide these individuals by ensuring that every individual recognizes and respects the individuality of every other. In acquiring this experience of the necessity of reciprocal recognition and respect, self-consciousness (in Hegel's exalted phrase) "steps out into the spiritual daylight of the present". This is so inasmuch as this reciprocal recognition culminates in the equality of all before the law.

After mankind, for thousands of years, had judged itself by two legal standards – with the stronger standing judge over the weaker and keeping him subjected – it became accepted, through the dialectical movement of self-consciousness, that every citizen should recognize every other as possessing equal rights, identify with him, and accord to him the same human dignity and legal recourse as himself. The dialectical resolution of the master-and-slave relation through mutual recognition can, then, be seen as the first step toward that typically modern "form of *Geist*" that is equality before the law.

The Dialectical Movement of World History

Just as the individual consciousness is propelled forward by its own contradictions, so too is the history of the world. Indeed, individual consciousness, world history and the divine *Weltgeist* are, at bottom, just different perspectives on one and the same dialectical unfolding of Reason, which never comes to rest. The *Weltgeist* tirelessly turns the wheel of history, even if there exist cultures, like the Chinese, that appear to remain untouched by it for a time:

> The universal Geist does not remain stationary [...] It may certainly be the case with a single nation that its culture, art, science – its intellectual activities as a whole – are at a standstill. This appears, perhaps, to be the case with the Chinese, for example, who may have been as far advanced in every respect two thousand years ago as now. But the Weltgeist does not sink into this rest of indifference [...] *for its activity is its life.*[34]

Hegel's Central Idea

And indeed even China, as we now know, was seized, around a hundred years after Hegel's death, by the dynamic of world history and became a modern industrial state:

> [...] History is a conscious, self-mediating process – Geist emptied out into Time [...]. This Becoming presents a slow-moving succession of forms of Geist, a gallery of images, each of which, endowed with all the riches of Geist, moves so slowly just because the Self has to penetrate and digest this entire wealth of its substance.[35]

In other words, the succession of the ages is described by Hegel as "slow-moving" because an enormous effort is required of the *Weltgeist* in order to bring forth and shape its whole rich substance – i.e. all peoples, nations, artworks, buildings, and pieces of music – in all their respective eras and then to develop these on into other eras. But this effort of the *Weltgeist* is not, for Hegel, a feat performed by some God enthroned on high who moves history on from some point outside it. Rather, it is the self-movement of dialectical Reason, driving itself onward by the motor of the contradictions that emerge in the consciousness of individual human beings. Hegel, indeed, can only speak of a *Weltgeist*, or "World-Spirit", at all insofar as he holds that history, in all its multiform movement, fulfils a higher meaning and serves a final end, or result:

> This result it is at which the process of the world's history has been continually aiming, and to which the sacrifices that have ever and anon been laid on the vast altar of the earth through the long lapse of the ages have been offered.[36]

Hegel raises here the thrilling question of the end and aim of world history. His answer is amazingly simple. This aim and purpose, at which epoch after epoch has been aiming, is freedom:

Hegel's Central Idea

> World history is the progress of the consciousness of freedom – a progress whose necessity we have to recognize.[37]

What has been at issue, then, throughout the whole unfolding of human history – from the age of savage tribes up to the forming of peoples, cultures, cities and nations – has been, basically, the idea of freedom. The unfolding of this idea in the consciousness of mankind has been global history's golden thread. It began in the early cultures of the Ancient East:

> The Orientals have not yet attained the knowledge that Geist – Man as such – is free; and because they do not know this, they are not free. They only know that one is free.[38]

In this ancient oriental world this "one that was free" was, as a rule, the despotic ruling monarch. The thought of freedom had not yet been developed as a thought, i.e. was not an object of consciousness. Only among the Greeks do we see a wish for true freedom beginning to emerge:

> The consciousness of freedom first arose among the Greeks; and therefore they were free. But they, and the Romans likewise, knew only that *some* are free – not Man as such. Not even Plato and Aristotle knew this.[39]

Thus, in the Greek city-states, the citizens were free and could choose their government, but there were also a large number of unfree, rightless slaves. Only "some" were free. Then finally – after many centuries of wars and struggles – the modern Christian nations attained to the progressive awareness that Man as Man is free, or, as Hegel, with his typical enthusiasm, expresses it:

Hegel's Central Idea

[...] that it is the freedom of Geist that constitutes (Man's) essence.⁴⁰

Hegel sees, then, the meaning of history in the progressive unfolding of freedom. Not just the slave's self-liberation in the phase of the "master-slave dialectic" but the whole of history steers step by step toward this end-point. What Hegel understands by "freedom", however, is not the unlimited satisfaction of the needs and wishes of the individual but rather the limited fulfilment of these needs and wishes by and through the state. Only the state, he says, with its laws, judges, and proper legislation, makes possible a free and self-determined life for its citizens and protects them from arbitrary rule. In his *Philosophy of Right* he describes why the state is so important. Without the state, insight into the fact that human beings are not destined to be slaves would be just an idealistic demand, just "*something which ought to be*":

> [...] That the ineligibility of the human being, in and for himself, for slavery should no longer be apprehended merely as something which ought to be is an insight which comes only when we recognize that the idea of freedom is truly present only as the state.[41]

As an example of how the lack of a state means a lack of freedom Hegel cites the confused period immediately after the French Revolution. France sank into chaos. There was arbitrary rule by terror and violence by marauding gangs. It was not until Napoleon re-established an ordered state and created a new rule of law with the introduction of his Code Civil that French citizens were once again able to move and act freely. Such historical experiences led Hegel to call the state the very embodiment of freedom:

"The state is the actuality of concrete freedom [...].⁴²"

Indeed, insofar as the state maintains the moral and ethical order, it can be understood, says Hegel, as a subject in its own right, a kind of living ethical organism:

"The state is the actuality of the ethical idea [...]. The state is [...] the *rational* in and for itself.⁴³"

And, as the authority instantiating ethics and reason, the state has the right also to curtail the freedom of a citizen, to condemn him for infringement of the law, even to lock him in prison, in order to secure freedom and moral order for all the other citizens.

Hegel's characterization of the state as the embodiment of rationality and morality sounds, indeed, plausible as regards its function in fighting crime. But it has one serious drawback: If ever an individual citizen happens to come into conflict with the state, then, according to Hegel's theory, the state must always be in the right. Because, on this account, every system of ethics or morality from which the citizen might derive the critical moral stance he adopts has necessarily to be founded in, and created by, the state.

In Hegel, then, we find no such civil right of resistance to the state as had been formulated by the English philosopher John Locke more than a hundred years before him. Nor did Hegel hold a very high opinion of the democratic polity that had been called for by Rousseau some fifty years before. Hegel did not believe "the people" to be capable yet of understanding the aims of the state, which necessarily transcend the interests of the individual, and choosing representatives suitable for serving these ends. He considered, therefore, the Prussian political system of the time – with its bicameral "estates" assemblies and its hereditary monarchy – to be the best possible form of state. In this Prussian polity, he argued, world history had achieved its highest "form of *Geist*"; the progressing consciousness of

Hegel's Central Idea

freedom had reached its summit in the enlightened Prussian constitutional state. For this reason it is often said that Hegel betrayed, once he was installed in Berlin as "Prussia's state philosopher", his earlier sympathies with the politically much more progressive ideas of the French Enlightenment writers. This has been charged by Karl Popper, for example. In his book *The Open Society and its Enemies* he accuses Hegel of having made himself, by granting to the state a moral primacy over the individual, a defender, before the fact, of later totalitarianism. But this criticism surely goes too far, since Hegel defined the moral role of the state very precisely, and in the spirit of liberalism. The Prussian constitution was finally to accord to the state's citizens that which, in the centuries-long work of world history, had crystallized out of the resolution of humanity's contradictions: the mutual recognition and legitimacy of human beings as free self-consciousnesses with equal rights before the law:

A human being *counts* as such *because he is a human being*, not because he is a Jew, Catholic, Protestant, German, Italian etc.[44]

The Self-Developing World-Spirit as God

The Absolute – that is to say, God – is not, for Hegel, as for Christianity, an eternal and all-powerful deity, there since before Creation, who judges men after their deaths. Rather, it is, in Hegel's view, only in and through human beings that God grows to become what He is. This is why worshipping Him in humility makes no sense. There is, says Hegel, no vast gulf between Man and God. The Absolute is with us always, in the dialectical movement of consciousness and in world history, and wishes to be so. And since this is so, the ceremonies of the Catholic church seemed to Hegel to be irrational and even ridiculous. Himself a Protestant, he mocked the Catholic ritual of Holy Communion. The "World-Spirit", he argued, has better ways of entering the mind and spirit of Man than through the eating of the so-called "host". It is nonsense, he claimed,

[…] that the host is honoured (as God) even as an external thing.[45]

Hegel goes on in these lectures to point out this conception of the host has the dangerous consequence for Catholics that "if a mouse eats of the host, both it and its excrements (must be) reverenced." When this remark of Hegel's became known the Church was outraged. Although his students defended him, Hegel was forced to make an official apology and take back his remark.

The Catholic church, indeed, quite generally rejected Hegel's idea of God. A "World-Spirit" that develops itself through Nature, humanity and world history was, in the church's eyes, a form of pagan pantheism, i.e. the doctrine that God moves and works as a dispersed force in everything, for example in every blade of grass. Hegel accepted this rejection by the Catholic church. But he sought recognition by Protestantism for many years – sadly, in vain.

This controversy about the communion host shows how far removed Hegel's idea of the Absolute was from the classical Christian idea of God. For him, God, Man and History are not three different things but rather a single force: that of the dialectical self-movement of *Geist*. This is why the cardinal thesis that Hegel arrives at in his philosophy is one which claims that Man can know God only insofar as God is present in Man's own thinking and doing so that, through this human thinking and doing, God learns something of Himself. Hegel's cardinal thesis here, in other words, is that God's self-consciousness is, in the last analysis, one and the same with the self-consciousness of Man, and vice versa:

Man knows God only insofar as God Himself knows Himself in Man. The Geist of Man whereby he knows God is simply the Geist of God Himself.[46]

It is only through progress in history and the millennial efforts of humanity that God "comes to Himself" and resolves His initial self-alienation:

The True is the whole. But the whole is nothing other than the essence consummating itself through its own development. Of the Absolute it must be said that it is essentially a result, that only in the *end* is it what it truly is […].[47]

Hegel's Central Idea

The "World-Spirit" – i.e. God – is realized through the forms of *Geist* that make up world history. Even events in Nature are expressions of this "World-Spirit" in a process of becoming. But what role in this is played by the human individual? Can he stand, with his free will, against the "World-Spirit"? Can his actions alter the course of history? Hegel's answer here appears at first to be a sobering one:

> The insight, then, to which [...] philosophy should lead us is that the actual world is as it ought to be, that the truly good, the universal divine Reason, is the power capable of actualizing itself.

> [...] God governs the world. The actual working of his government – the carrying out of his plan – is the history of the world.[48]

If God governs the world and world history is the carrying out of his plan, what power of decision is left to individuals? How can individual dialectical reason be reconciled with the Providence of the "World-Spirit"? Or, conversely, how can we believe in a plan on the part of the "World-Spirit" when it is clear that, in history, politicians have always taken decisions and conquerors like Caesar or Napoleon have surely changed history's course?

The Cunning of Reason

Hegel was aware, of course, of the influence of great personalities on history. He even speaks of "world-historical individuals" and describes them as acting practically and so as to meet the political needs of the day, without reference to any such thing as a "World-Spirit". But they thereby indirectly serve the greater whole:

> Such individuals have no consciousness of the Idea as such. They are practical and political men. [...] They gratify their own interests, but something more is thereby accomplished which is [...] not present in their consciousness and not included in their design.[49]

Hegel's Central Idea

Individuals like Alexander the Great, Caesar or Napoleon often pursued interests of their own without having any overview of the broader course of history. But they left their mark on their eras and carried history forward, inasmuch as they saw what needed to be done at that specific moment:

[...] They were thinking men who had insight into the requirements of the time.[50]

Napoleon, for example, caused to occur in history exactly what the time and the "World-Spirit" required, inasmuch as, in Hegel's view, it had been high time in France that the decadent state built around the royal court, and the king himself, were stripped of their power. It had also been high time, after centuries of feudalism and of laws being made in their own interest by feudal lords, for Napoleon to realize throughout Europe, by the introduction of constitutions and a general "Civil Code", the idea of equality before the law. It was for this reason that Hegel wrote in his diary, on seeing Napoleon riding by the window of his home in Jena just as he was composing the final pages of the *Phenomenology*:

I saw the Emperor – this World-Soul – riding out of the city on reconnaissance.[51]

For Hegel Napoleon was indeed a "World-Soul", a man who fulfilled the "World-Spirit". He himself may have wished, primarily, only to extend his own power and fame and secure his imperial throne. But what remained of him after his banishment to St. Helena was the dialectically overdue renewal of Europe as regards its citizens` equality before the law. In this sense, Napoleon was, as Hegel says, a "manager" or "instrument of the World-Spirit". Though pursuing, perhaps, only his own ambition and passions, he served thereby the development of Reason and the "World-Spirit":

> This may be called the *cunning of Reason* - that it sets the passions to work for itself.[52]

The "World-Spirit" applies "cunning" inasmuch as, while allowing human beings to freely decide how to act, it uses their passions and their actions to push on Reason's development in each succeeding epoch. In this respect, each stage of development has its justification and its truth. Even the benighted Middle Ages, with its superstitions and witch-burnings, was a "form of *Geist*" which had necessarily to emerge and had, for a time, its truth:

> Therefore, I declared to myself from the start [...] that Reason rules the world and has likewise ruled world history.[53]

Since the *Weltgeist*, through its dialectical self-movement, drives the development of Reason onward from epoch to epoch, each epoch must, on its own terms, be rational. This is the source and basis of Hegel's provocative claim that:

What is rational is actual, and what is actual is rational.[54]

Both certain contemporaries of Hegel and many later philosophers have violently criticized Hegel for making this claim, since it appears to be one that can be used to excuse any kind of wrong and injustice in the world. If everything that "actually" happens, however bad, must be called rational, then one loses any standard by which the world as it is might be criticized. And indeed Hegel does consider even states which are dictatorially governed to be necessary stages on Reason's long path to full self-development:

Each nation [...] has the constitution appropriate and proper to it.[55]

In the context of Hegel's thought this does not, indeed, mean that dictatorships, being bad and backward state constitutions, need, in principle, just to be accepted. Precisely the dialectical movement of consciousness can, once the right time has come around, take up a negating stance to any injustice and transform it into its dialectical opposite. Any such relief of one "form of *Geist*" by another, however, will inevitably involve conflicts. World history, as it moves on, cannot pay any regard to people's personal happiness:

The history of the world is not the theatre of happiness. Periods of happiness are blank pages in it, for they are periods of harmony, periods when the antithesis is in abeyance.[56]

Since world history drives itself on by means of its own contradictions, the phases of conflict and contestation tend to be longer than the phases of harmony and consolidation. It is the task of the individual to recognize the signs of the times and to collaborate in the necessary progress of the consciousness of freedom. Even if the final goal of history and the operation of the "World-Spirit" are not clear to him, this individual knows what to do. He knows this because he does not make his decisions in some empty, neutral space but rather, as a child of his time, can, indeed must, place himself in relation to this time.

The Final Goal of History

Where does history end? Is there a goal we are moving toward? Hegel's answer is clear and concise. There is such a goal, and it is one we cannot fail to reach, since it arrives of necessity and by itself:

But the goal is as necessarily fixed for knowledge as the serial progression;

Hegel's Central Idea

> it is the point where knowledge no longer needs to go beyond itself, where knowledge finds itself.[57]

Our knowledge, which carries on growing from epoch to epoch, has, at the end of its long dialectical movement from primitive "sense-certainty" up to modern self-consciousness, one last important experience. It finally recognizes itself as the dialectical movement of the "Absolute Spirit" that it had really been from the beginning. It is at this point that "knowledge no longer needs to go beyond itself". It has arrived at its goal. It can no longer rise above itself or drive itself beyond itself because there are no more contradictions to overcome. It is now, as Hegel writes:

> [...] Absolute knowing, or Geist that knows itself in the shape of Geist [...].[58]

The "forms of *Geist*" succeed and relieve one another until the total development of the "World-Spirit", and at the same time the total development of individual thinking, has been achieved – namely, in a brilliant final resolution and reconciliation of all contradictions in Absolute Knowing or, as Hegel also phrases it, in "the Absolute Notion":

> The realm of Spirits (Geister) which is formed in this way in the outer world […] constitutes a succession in Time in which one Geist relieved another of its charge and each took over the empire of the world from its predecessor. Their goal is the revelation of the depth of Spirit, and this is the *Absolute Notion* […].⁵⁹

But what does this mean, concretely, for the individual? In the Absolute Notion – or Absolute Knowing – there is achieved, Hegel argues, a reconciliation in three respects. Firstly, there is a reconciliation of the individual with society. If, in primitive times,

Hegel's Central Idea

the individual experienced his fellow men as beings strange and exterior to him, he now identifies with them. He knows that it is only through the recognition of others that he can achieve self-recognition and that their freedom implies his own. Consciousness has acquired, in the course of world history, the experience that, although it is independent and free, it can remain so over time only if it is recognized as such by another free and independent consciousness. Consciousness recognizes itself as

'I' that is 'we' and 'we' that is 'I'.[60]

Whereas at the beginning of history life had been "a war of all against all" and "man a wolf to man", with each barbaric tribe battling every other, we arrive, at history's end, at a general mutual reconciliation. The individual now knows himself to be a part of the whole, part of a species. The pure concept of recognition is brought to realization. Human beings recognize themselves as reciprocally recognizing individuals.

Secondly, the individual, at history's end, is also reconciled with what Hegel calls "substance". By "substance" Hegel does not just mean Nature and physical matter; he also means such things as peoples, states and institutions. This is why he can say that everything which had appeared to us, at the beginning of history, to be so recalcitrant, savage and alien becomes, at history's end, part of the dialectical self-movement of our own consciousness. The *Geist* (mind and spirit) of Man knows itself to be both subject and "substance" at the same time, since it recognizes itself to be something essentially extended throughout substance. Hegel formulates this as follows:

This last becoming of Geist, *Nature*, is its living, immediate becoming. Nature, being externalized Geist, is in its existence nothing but [...] the movement which reinstates the *Subject*.[61]

Hegel's Central Idea

This idea that Nature is externalized *Geist*, and that we come to recognize in the end, through Absolute Knowing, that the dialectical movement of the thinking subject moves Nature as well and has always moved it, can be understood, with certain qualifications, in the following terms: Today, Man recognizes himself not only in and as *homo sapiens* but in the whole process of Nature that has created Man as what he is. We recognize ourselves as both subject and substance of that millions-of-years-long self-movement of evolution, from single-celled to multi-celled organisms up to *homo erectus* and on to our present form. Today, every schoolchild knows that the human mind is also a product of Nature. But Hegel says more than this. Once we have reached the last and highest stage of Absolute Knowing and recognized ourselves, in our dialectical thinking, to be the motor of world history and of the processes of Nature, it suddenly becomes clear to us that there can be nothing, and never has been anything, outside of our thought:

> Comprehended in this is the fact that Being is Thought.[62]

Hegel is able to propose such a radical thesis because, as he sees it, Being – that is to say, reality in its entirety – can, in any case, only enter our awareness through our own dialectical thought. Nothing is real except through our thinking of it. Because what we cannot grasp with our thoughts – that is to say, with our consciousness – does not exist, or at least we know nothing about it. This is why we can recognize, once we have reached the stage of Absolute Knowing, that all reality, even if it should initially appear as something strange to us, is, in the last analysis, a product of our own thought, so that we are indeed "subject" and "substance" at once.

Thirdly and lastly, the individual is also reconciled with the "World-Spirit". In primitive times God appeared to us to be an all-powerful being inspiring fear – a being situated quite outside of ourselves, requiring worship and the bringing of sacrifices. Now we know that God is, and always was, only the movement of world history coming to itself in the form of progress in the consciousness of freedom:

Consciousness [...] recognizes God therein.[63]

Hegel's Central Idea

God no longer floats above us, waiting to punish us or save us after our death, but has rather brought Himself forth in and through human consciousness in the course of the long labour of world history. He has trodden this way together with us and, like us, grown thereby. Since He too is at once subject and substance, among the forms of His self-actualization, at the end of history, are just and rational institutions such as the modern constitutional state.

This is why Hegel can write so enthusiastically about the state as the actualization of the "World-Spirit" and say that the idea of the state is a divine one. Certain individual states, indeed, may appear far from divine, but:

In considering the Idea of the state, we must not have any particular states or particular institutions in mind; instead, we should consider the Idea, this actual God, in its own right.[64]

The state, then, marks an end point to dialectics; it is "actual(ized) God" or, as Hegel also puts it:

> [...] the form which (Geist's) complete realization assumes in external existence.[65]

But Hegel believed that it was not just historical and political development that had reached its crowning conclusion in his own age of enlightened absolutism; philosophy too, he was convinced, had achieved, in his own teachings, the last and highest of all its possible "forms of *Geist*". He was, admittedly, modest enough to state that, though he was saying "philosophy's last word", he was not doing so just by his own merit.

The dialectical development itself, he argued, had raised him to this throne, inasmuch as his philosophy of *Geist* formed the necessary resolution of the last and greatest contradiction in the long history of philosophy. For centuries the rationalists and theologians had interpreted everything on the earth as just a gift of God's. Man himself had been understood as a mere copy, made in God's image. Philosophers, in other words, had been concerned always only to understand God, whether it be under the name of God or under that of the Absolute or the Celestial. We see, says Hegel:

> [...] a strenuous, almost over-zealous and frenzied effort to tear men away from their preoccupation with the sensuous, from their ordinary, private affairs, and to direct their gaze to the stars [...].

> The meaning of all that is hung on the thread of light by which it was linked to that heaven. Instead of dwelling in this world's presence, men looked beyond it, following this thread to an other-worldly presence, so to speak.[66]

Once science, and humanity as a whole, had finally understood that one makes no progress in the discovery of truth if one conceives of it as lying in some celestial "beyond", a radical counter-movement emerged. Modern empiricism, in Hegel's view, was the negation of all that was celestial. The empiricists rejected the idea that events on earth could be explained through some notion of the final unity of everything in God. They replaced the former exclusive attention to "the beyond" with an attention to the "here-below", arguing that it was empirical experience alone – i.e. concrete experience that was experimentally repeatable – that formed a solid basis for the acquisition of knowledge. Philosopers like Bacon and Hume insisted that all true knowledge was derived from perception of the earthly world and always stayed bound to this latter. But in Hegel's view this purely materialist viewpoint, which stayed focussed on sensually perceptible, worldly matters alone, was also an impoverishment of true knowledge, since it left Man's thirst for discovering a meaning to life unassuaged:

> Now we seem to need just the opposite: sense is so fast rooted in earthly things […] and Geist shows itself as so impoverished that, like a wanderer in the desert craving for a mere mouthful of water, it seems to crave, for its refreshment, only the bare feeling of the Divine in general.[67]

Hegel believed that he had, with his own philosophy, resolved this contradiction between the last two great philosophical stances, whereby truth was sought on the one hand just in a pure thinking of the Absolute and on the other hand in visible objects and in experiments alone. Because the empirical insights acquired through scientific experiments are, in the end, one and the same with the experiences that emerge from the dialectical self-movement of *Geist* – i.e. Absolute Knowing in its process of arisal. Thus the Absolute and the empirical are reconciled with one another. Already at the very beginning of his philosophical career, the young Hegel had set himself great goals:

> To help bring philosophy closer to the form of Science – to the goal where it can lay aside the title '*love* of knowing' and be *actual knowing* – this is what I have set myself to do.[68]

Hegel wanted to make of philosophy a science in the sense of turning what had, since the Greeks, been called mere "love of truth" or "love of wisdom" (*philosophia*) into an actual "knowing of what is true". And indeed, he attempted, with his philosophy of *Geist*, to give definitive answers to all philosophical questions. Having arrived at the end of history, Hegel argued, we can finally cease speculating and posing further questions because we know now that God, Man, Nature and History are all only expressions of one and the same movement of thought which we have been involved in since history's beginning and which the human mind and soul now recognizes as its own inmost essence:

From the chalice of this realm of Spirits foams forth for him his own infinitude.[69]

Of What Use is Hegel's Discovery for Us Today?

Is There Reason in History or Has the "World-Spirit" Failed Us?

It sounds strange to us today if we are told that we stand, at the present time, at the end of history and in the midst of a great celebration of reconciliation – with Nature, with God, with our fellow men and with the entire world. Too many problems and conflicts still weigh upon our present era for us to be able to share Hegel's optimism.

Hegel's idea of the world's history as a constant process of Reason's development and consummation attracted, indeed, the scorn already of some of his contemporaries, such as Schopenhauer. But it was the experience of the 20th Century, with its two world wars, that really shook any belief that Europeans might have held in "Reason in history" as Hegel argued for it. The German philosopher Adorno, for example, raised the provocative question: can we, after Auschwitz, still speak of progress in history at all? And we do have to face the fact that, despite all the cosmopolitan ideas expounded by Hegel, Kant, Rousseau and Locke, and the whole centuries-long European tradition of Enlightenment, such an act of barbarism did once again occur in the heart of Europe? Nationalism and racism led to two world wars in which the citizens of England, France, Germany, Italy and almost every nation in the world tried to kill each other. How was such a thing possible? Did dialectical Reason let us down after all? Can one – after the massive setbacks suffered by our civilization, such as global warming, the irremediable pollution caused by atomic waste, and the capitalist crisis – still speak of "Reason in history"?

In Adorno's view, the answer was clearly: 'no'. If, he argued, there had ever been a "World-Spirit" which had formed and guided history in the paths of Reason, it had certainly ceased to do so in the modern era. Enlightenment itself had been a double-edged process which had resulted in Reason, Hegel's 'motor of history', transforming itself into Unreason. Hegel had simply been wrong in thinking that Reason would go on developing and permeating the world. To Hegel's "the True is the whole" Adorno opposed the view that, in a world colonized and manipulated by nationalism and capitalism, "the whole is the False."

Of What Use is Hegel's Discovery for Us Today?

Hegel died in 1831 and so never had to experience nationalism, fascism, or their consequence, the Holocaust. But he would surely have insisted that such setbacks, terrible as they may be, are nonetheless also necessary contradictions on the path of Reason's self-development. Because even nationalism, racism and fascism, Hegel might have argued, were only passing "forms of *Geist*" whose dialectical resolution eventually gave rise to the "form of *Geist*" that is our present united Europe. These doctrines had necessarily, according to Hegel's logic, to fail because they created their own contradiction, their own antithesis, which inevitably led to their self-dissolution.

Hegel would argue that nations that draw their consciousness of their own selfhood from the negation or denigration of the selfhood of others are doomed to founder on the contradiction that such a manner of acquiring self-consciousness can never be reciprocal. Because a people that seeks its truth in the displacement, oppression or even extermination of other peoples thereby provokes an existential "war of all against all" and, by denying the principle of states' right to existence, also denies its own. The "truth", then, of nationalism and racism leads necessarily to conflict between nations; it thus proves itself to be "untruth" and is negated and resolved in that higher "form of *Geist*" that is the reciprocal recognition of nations and states.

This resolution of the nationalistic and racist "form of *Geist*" within a new European self-understanding has now become a "form of *Geist*" in its own right. It is nowadays unthinkable that citizens of France, England and Germany should once again try to kill each other. Today – although just two or three generations ago France and Germany were considered by many to be "traditional foes" – nothing is more natural than young citizens of both countries studying and working in the other.

That this old enmity seems definitively overcome, and that Europeans now reciprocally recognize their liberty and national sanctity, is an indication that Hegel's conviction that history is rational, and consists in a "progressively greater consciousness of freedom", may stand against Adorno's criticism after all. Hegel would surely even today stick by his central idea that:

The only thought which philosophy brings with it to the contemplation

Of What Use is Hegel's Discovery for Us Today?

> of history is the simple conception of Reason: that *Reason* is the sovereign of the world; that the history of the world, therefore, presents us with a rational process. This conviction and intuition is a *hypothesis* in the domain of history as such.[70]

For Hegel, then, the belief that "the history of the world presents us with a rational process" is a hypothesis that we must adopt if we are to have any hope of understanding history at all. If one were to proceed on the contrary assumption that the course of history is something irrational and senseless, then all historical events would just be random, absurd fortuities in a lottery. The fact, however, that we can talk of "spirits of the age", of epochs, and of traditions already speaks in favour of Hegel's assumption that there is some sort of logic at work in history.

And in fact no one today would seriously maintain that historical events are merely random. To this extent, Hegel's thesis that progress, or a development of Reason, is recognizable in history despite all setbacks is a plausible one. Whether this development always takes Hegel's triadic form of thesis, antithesis and synthesis remains open to question but there is surely some truth is his discovery that each epoch builds upon the last.

But of what use is this discovery to us? What practical consequences does it have? Can we simply sit back and watch Reason unfold in society?

To Think Dialectically is to Think Critically

In the end, Hegel's philosophy allows just one answer: we can and must, as individuals, ourselves push on Reason in history. We can illustrate this by the concrete example of a famous remark by the last President of the Soviet Union, Mikhail Gorbachev: "Life punishes those who delay".

This remark is in fact a striking expression of Hegel's teachings regarding the interplay of individual consciousness and "World-Spirit". It is, indeed, only on the basis of Hegelian thinking that the remark makes full sense. For although, on the one hand, the individual is free to act or not to act, he will, on the other hand, if he does not promptly do what Reason requires, surely be overtaken by life's changes – that is, by the historical "World-Spirit" – and suffer the consequences. The remark, then, might well have run: "History punishes those who delay".

It was to Erich Honecker, the last head of state of the socialist republic established in the eastern half of a divided Germany, that Gorbachev spoke these words. At the time he said them, there was already great discontent among East German citizens with the bureaucrats of the authoritarian ruling party. Gorbachev had already recognized that the socialist planned economy not just in East Germany but in the Soviet Union itself needed to be reformed. With his programme of *perestroika* he introduced an era of democratization and market reforms and ended the long East-West conflict. But Honecker refused to heed him and held stubbornly to the socialist planned economy until he was finally overtaken by history and driven from power by his own people.

In this light we can answer the question of whether we can, as individuals, help form history and push on Reason's development. We can and must! Gorbachev, for example, recognized the historical situation and acted rationally. He ended the arms race, thus perhaps saving the world from atomic war. He was surely a "world-historical individual" in Hegel's sense who, going against the bureaucrats of his own party, did what he thought right and what, as Hegel would, say, "the time demanded". The course of history, then, surely is something that depends on our commitment to the cause of Reason. The many East German citizens who marched in the streets for freedom also brought about change by brave action. But if it is Man, in the end, who makes history, is the "World-Spirit" not a superfluous assumption?

The philosopher Ludwig Feuerbach interpreted Hegel in just this way. He argued that Hegel had rendered his own use of the "God" idea superfluous by stating that Man's knowledge of God was, in the end, nothing other than Man's self-knowledge. This raises the question of whether the "World-Spirit" can simply be dropped from Hegel's philosophy as a redundant phantom.

No, it cannot, as we can see by the example of Erich Honecker. The influence exerted by the consciousness of an individual is limited; that of historical Reason, though, is unlimited. Honecker, for example, despite his use of police, army and secret service, had no chance of halting the wheel of history. He could no longer suppress the new truth. The citizens' urge toward freedom was too great and the time was ripe for change. Reason asserts itself in history even when the powerful refuse to recognize it. Or, as Hegel says:

We must hold to the conviction that it is the nature of truth to prevail when its time has come [...].[71]

History, then, decidedly does have, vis-à-vis the individual and his decisions, a life and dynamic of its own. This is why Hegel speaks of the operation of the rational "World-Spirit" which, as a tenacious aspiration toward Reason, is more than just the sum of the individual deeds and thoughts emerging on earth. Hitler, for example, found many supporters for his vision. Since, however, "it is the nature of truth to prevail", and Hitler's vision constituted no progress in the consciousness of freedom, this vision was bound to fail in the end. The "World-Spirit", being the development of Reason, is not impressed by numbers. The notion of a "thousand-year Reich" for "the Aryan race" was (one might say with Hegel) refuted by history, the "World-Spirit", in just six years – although the distress and misery of this aberration will remain preserved, even in its negation, in the consciousness of the nations forever.

The "World-Spirit", then, is, in the end, nothing else than the tenacious aspiration of Reason to prevail whenever the time is ripe for it to do so. But since people, due to their passions, do not always recognize when the time is ripe, Hegel distinguishes between the "World-Spirit" and the spirit or mind of individuals, even if both follow the same dialectic and, at the end of history, the individual too recognizes himself in the movement of the "World-Spirit".

Just because there are always setbacks in history, it is our task to help Reason along in its self-development, to recognize truth, or, as Hegel says, to do what is necessary in order that a new, higher "form of *Geist*" relieves the old one. It is important, says Hegel, for human beings:

[...] To know the [...] necessary, directly sequent step in progress which their world (is) to take, to make this their aim, and to expend their energy in promoting it.[72]

It is the task of the individual, then, to recognize the signs of the times and not to rest content with what has already been historically achieved – because what seemed to be truth in one period may very shortly afterward become just a shadow of truth. Thus, for example, whereas mankind's entry into the Atomic Age was not long ago celebrated as the dawn of a new era of prosperity, this "truth" has since, due to the various catastrophes and difficulties arising from atomic power, sunk to the status of a mere shadow of the truth. Thanks to citizen protests an antithesis was formed whereby atomic energy rather endangered than secured the basis of society's existence. As the synthesis within this dialectical process certain states in Europe and Asia have begun to replace atomic with renewable energies. But this synthesis in its turn is already becoming a new dialectical thesis. The new form of providing energy has, for example, led to a massive increase in the cultivation of rapeseed to make organic petrol which in turn led to food shortages. This new contradiction requires new solutions.

Thus consciousness, for Hegel, drives itself ever onward by the motor of its own contradictions. But what does this mean concretely? To think dialectically is to think critically. We must repeatedly adopt the stance of negation and probe and question what exists.

To Live Means to Change

With his dialectics Hegel does not just provide us with an important tool in times of social change requiring decisive acts of contradiction. Also in the private sphere insight into "becoming" can play an important role. Life means constant change. It is part of our very nature, for example, that we grow up and older and are constantly faced with new challenges. A child has different problems from an adolescent or an adult. The world around us also changes rapidly. But through our capacity for dialectical thinking we can meet these challenges and generate new truths. Because something that, in one phase of our lives, we thought entirely reasonable we can often, a few years later, look on as unreasonable, replacing it by another truth. As Hegel says:

Truth is its own self-movement.[73]

That we need in life constantly to re-think the things that we once held to be absolutely true doesn't mean one shouldn't struggle to keep what one already has. Naturally, one does not wish to lose one's life's companion or one's job, or to have to get by without things one has become attached to. Nor does one wish to see young people make mistakes that might have been avoided. But if changes come, one must deal with them – and it is here that Hegel's philosophy of *Geist* can be an important help. Hegel teaches us to understand life as a process and to see the truth that we hold to at any particular time as what it is: a "form of *Geist*" which helps us to understand and to handle our present world but which is apt, by its very nature, to be replaced by some new form and which from time to time even must be so replaced. We should allow the truth of this insight – and not just as an abstract idea but as a concrete approach to life which we need to adopt as the basis of the way we look at the world and our fellow men.

Living also means accepting the changes that come with age. It makes no sense to hold to the belief that one will stay forever young. If one admits that everything has its time, it is easier to handle the approach of old age and its frailties and to pass on responsibility to the young generation. Even in youth, however, crises can be better handled by applying that dialectical approach of *Aufheben* which we have discussed above: putting an end, indeed, to an unsatisfactory condition, but doing so only by using said condition to transform oneself as well as it, thus raising everything onto a new and higher level. Germany's greatest writer, Goethe, once asked Hegel to explain to him in simple words just what dialectics is. Hegel told him that it is "nothing other than that spirit of contradiction, well regulated and methodically formed, that dwells in every man." This spirit of contradiction, inherent in all of us, needs to be lived out because it opens up for us the opportunity for self-development.

By showing that we move on not through the abolition of what exists but through its *Aufheben* – its abolition, preservation and raising up onto a higher level all at once – Hegel also conveys the important life-lesson that for a change to occur – be it in private or in professional life – does not mean that all that one had before the change is lost. All this old truth remains, in Hegel's phrase, *aufgehoben* in the new. Even death – which Hegel calls "the most dreadful of non-actualities" – can be aufgehoben in this way, dialectically, by the human faculty of understanding, despite how strenuous it is to even think of it:

Of What Use is Hegel's Discovery for Us Today?

Death, if that is what we want to call this non-actuality, is of all things the most dreadful, and to hold fast to what is dead requires the greatest strength.[74]

In daily life we tend to repress the thought of death as something that puts too great a strain on our understanding. It does not fit well with an optimistic, active attitude. But Hegel urges us not to avert our mental gaze here:

But the life of Geist is not the life that shrinks from death [...] but rather the life that endures it and maintains itself in it.[75]

The human mind does in fact possess the power to transform the negativity of death into living Being:

> It is this power [...] only by looking the negative in the face and tarrying with it. This tarrying with the negative is the magical power that converts it into Being.[76]

By looking death in the face and admitting to ourselves that we must die, we can use this very insight into the fact that death limits our personal possibilities to inspire ourselves to lead a resolute life and make good use of the time we have. What is more, our own consciousness – and this is the comfort that Hegel also offers us – remains *aufgehoben* (preserved, even if cancelled out) after our physical death in the continuing development of universal *Geist*. Hegel promises us, instead of an afterlife in the beyond, one in the here-below of the steadily progressing *Weltgeist*. Since our individual consciousness itself consists in the dialectical self-development of Reason, we participate even after death in the continuous self-unfolding of the rational "World-Spirit". Our commitment to life, our efforts and the knowledge we acquire, are not lost but are preserved, transformed, in the shape of a living legacy passed down to the "forms of *Geist*" of later generations. Even those of us who are not world-historical individuals who pass into history books also make ourselves immortal through our personal commitments, be this to the raising of children, the passing-on of knowledge, or just the performance of the necessary work of society.

Hegel for Managers

The heart of global capitalism is the Stock Exchange, or, in other words, the trade in shares. At many such Exchanges there are to be found two statues: of a bull and of a bear. The bull symbolizes the spirit of the stock market in periods when share prices are rising and people buy with confidence and aggression; the bear symbolizes periods when prices fall and traders sell and retreat to secured positions, like bears to their lairs.

It is not hard to see that not only share prices but our whole economic life is characterized by this peculiar dialectic of phases of growth and boom followed by phases of stagnation and recession. Over-production gives rise to economic contraction. The global economy too, then, drives itself onward by the motor of its own contradictions. All political or economic attempts to render this dialectic less socially painful through measures to stimulate or stabilize the economy have hope of succeeding only when those who initiate them correctly read the signs of the times.

Likewise, it is extremely important for managers to react to the constant changes in the markets with alterations in the range of products a company offers, or, better still, to anticipate such changes. This is why large firms often employ creative minds whose sole task consists in adopting a stance of negation vis-à-vis the firm's own corporate philosophy and thinking out strategies and products that run counter to it. Thus Mercedes, for example – a car manufacturer renowned for selling luxurious grey-black saloon cars to the fashionable elite – at one point brought a modest compact car, available in a range of colours, onto the market and acquired, with this appropriately-named "Smart" range of products, a whole new group of customers.

It is also said that the founder of the successful US firm Carnival Cruise Line, with its trademark "Fun Ships", proceeded in the best Hegelian manner of concrete negation in order to arrive at his business

Of What Use is Hegel's Discovery for Us Today?

concept. First he noted down on a piece of paper all that one usually thinks of when cruise ships are mentioned: rich, exclusive, mostly old or middle-aged passengers; evening dress; orchestras; dinner at the captain's table etc. Then he noted down all that contradicted these things: accessibility for all, including young and modestly-earning people; casual clothing; self-service canteens, discos. And for a business concept based on this spirit of contradiction he found many investors. There are currently more than 30 such "Fun Ships" plying the ocean waves and achieving massive profits. This is surely another case of someone's (in Hegel's phrase) "recognizing the signs of the times".

A dialectical approach has long been part of the very ABC of advertising and marketing professionals. One of the first things learnt by such professionals is never to bore their public and to adopt, wherever possible, a stance of contradiction vis-à-vis established advertising messages and the cultural standards behind them. Thus the energy-drink firm Red Bull chose to advertise its product not by claims that it was healthy, tasty, quenched thirst etc. but rather with claims contradictory to these: that it was adventurous, dangerous, and even "gave wings". There are no limits set to the dialectical imagination.

Using Hegel to Go Beyond Hegel

Hegel's discovery that reality is a constant process of change and "becoming" was surely a great achievement, likewise his analysis of history as the development of Reason in the sense of freedom's self-actualization. But Hegel's understanding and celebration of the Prussian state as it existed in his own lifetime as the highest and fullest embodiment of this developing historical Reason must nonetheless pose a problem for us today. Equally problematical seems his conviction that his own philosophy was the last and highest form of human thought that could never be superseded.

Nowadays we know that, tolerant and well-functioning as the Prussian state of Hegel's lifetime may have been when measured by the standard of the day, it represented just a first modest step toward modern democracy. We also, of course, know that Hegel's system was by no means philosophy's last, decisive word.

It must be admitted, then, that Hegel was led into error by serious overestimation both of his era and of his own self. Does this mean that his key notion of constant change has been invalidated? Can we dismiss Hegel as a relic of intellectual history?

What is true is that Hegel himself did not live up to this insight into constant change that he had given to the world. But the insight itself stands all the firmer for just this reason. We remain greatly enriched by his discovery of the dimension of "becoming".

If Hegel has bequeathed to us something we can benefit from, then it is the reminder always to be attentive to change and development in history and in our own lives. It remains our task not to rest content with the world as it exists but rather constantly to be negating, so as to raise development to higher levels. Every change harbours the possibility of improvement. This applies both to the private and in the broader social sphere.

If we are to draw the full benefit, then, from Hegel's discovery of "the dimension of becoming", we need to use Hegel to go beyond Hegel. We go, indeed, beyond the point where Hegel himself halted whenever we admit that, as Hegel stated, each epoch is just a stone in the mosaic of the great process of Reason's self-development:

> World history is the progress of the consciousness of freedom – a progress whose necessity we have to recognize.[77]

For the sake of this progress we need, and are able to, develop, for each age, a dialectical imagination. To think dialectically is to think critically. The German author Bertolt Brecht recognized what explosive force inhered in the dialectical movement of thought. In his poem *In Praise of Dialectics* he urges people to believe, above all in periods of distress and oppression, in the power of dialectical change:

> Whoever is still alive must never say 'never!'
> Certainty is never certain.
> It will not stay the way it is.
> When the rulers have spoken
> Then the ruled will begin to speak [...]
> How can he who has recognized his condition ever be stopped?
> Because the vanquished of today will be tomorrow's victors
> And 'never!' will become 'this very day!'[78]

Of What Use is Hegel's Discovery for Us Today?

Even if Hegel himself succumbed to the illusion that his own age was the crown and end of Reason's self-development, he bequeathed to us, nonetheless, the lasting heritage of his discovery that being is endless "becoming". Such a heritage is also a challenge to us to play an active role in a self-development of Reason that is plainly still going on; to adopt a negating, critical stance toward what presently counts as truth; and to tirelessly apply the force of our understanding to distinguishing the true from the self-contradictory:

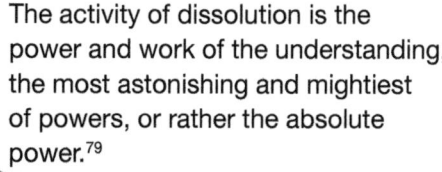

The activity of dissolution is the power and work of the understanding, the most astonishing and mightiest of powers, or rather the absolute power.[79]

Bibliographical References:

1. Georg Wilhelm Friedrich Hegel, Elements of the Philosophy of Right, edited by Allen W. Wood and translated by H. B. Nisbet, Cambridge University Press, 1991, p. 20.
2. Arthur Schopenhauer, The World as Will and Idea, translated by R. B. Haldane and J. Kemp, Routledge & Kegan Paul Ltd. 1883, Vol. 2, p. 22.
3. Will Durant, The Story of Philosophy, Garden City Publishing, New York, 1933, p. 320.
4. Hegel, Phenomenology of Spirit, translated by A. V. Miller, Oxford University Press, Oxford, 1977, p. 11.
5. Hegel, Lectures on the History of Philosophy, translated by E. S. Haldane, Kegan, Paul, Trench, Truebner and Co. London, 1892. Vol 1 p. 53; also found in: Reading Hegel: The Introductions edited by Aakash Singh and Rimina Mohapatra, re.press, Melbourne, Australia, 2008, p. 230.
6. Hegel, Phenomenology of Spirit, translated by A. V. Miller, Oxford University Press, Oxford, 1977, p. 17
7. Hegel, Lectures on the History of Philosophy, translated by E. S. Haldane, Kegan, Paul, Trench, Truebner and Co. London, 1892. Vol 1 p. 22; also to be found in: Reading Hegel: The Introductions edited by Aakash Singh and Rimina Mohapatra, re.press, Melbourne, Australia, 2008, p. 226.
8. Hegel, The Science of Logic, translated and edited by George Di Giovanni, Cambridge University Press 2010, p. 382
9. Hegel, The Philosophy of History, New York, 1956, translated by J. Sibree, p. 557.
10. Hegel, Phenomenology of Spirit, translated by A. V. Miller, Oxford University Press, Oxford, 1977, pps. 492
11. Hegel, Lectures on the History of Philosophy, translated by E. S. Haldane, Kegan, Paul, Trench, Truebner and Co. London, 1892. Vol 1 p. 2; also to be found in: Reading Hegel: The Introductions edited by Aakash Singh and Rimina Mohapatra, re.press, Melbourne, Australia, 2008, p. 223.
12. Hegel, Introduction to Lectures on the Philosophy of History,

in: Reading Hegel: The Introductions edited by Aakash Singh and Rimina Mohapatra, re.press, Melbourne, Australia, 2008, p. 142.
13 Hegel, Lectures on the History of Philosophy, translated by E. S. Haldane, Kegan, Paul, Trench, Truebner and Co. London, 1892. Vol 1 p. 3.
14 Hegel, Phenomenology of Spirit, translated by A. V. Miller, Oxford University Press, Oxford, 1977, p. 55.
15 Hegel, The Science of Logic, translated and edited by George Di Giovanni, Cambridge University Press 2010, pps. 81-82.
16 Ibid.
17 Ibid. p. 382
18 Ibid. p. 381
19 Ibid. pps. 381-2
20 Ibid. p. 33
21 Ibid.
22 Hegel, Phenomenology of Spirit, translated by A. V. Miller, Oxford University Press, Oxford, 1977, p. 27.
23 Ibid.
24 Ibid. p. 17.
25 Ibid. p. 110
26 Ibid. p. 112
27 Ibid. p. 116
28 Ibid. p. 117
29 Ibid. p. 118
30 Ibid. p. 118-9
31 Ibid. p. 118
32 Ibid. p. 112
33 Ibid. p. 110
34 Hegel, Lectures on the History of Philosophy, translated by E. S. Haldane, Kegan, Paul, Trench, Truebner and Co. London, 1892. Vol 1 p. 3
35 Hegel, Phenomenology of Spirit, translated by A. V. Miller, Oxford University Press, Oxford, 1977, p. 492.
36 Hegel, Introduction to Lectures on the Philosophy of History, in: Reading Hegel: The Introductions edited by Aakash Singh and Rimina Mohapatra, re.press, Melbourne, Australia, 2008, p. 122.
37 Ibid.
38 Ibid. p. 121.

39 Ibid. pps. 121-122
40 Ibid.
41 Georg Wilhelm Friedrich Hegel, Elements of the Philosophy of Right, edited by Allen W. Wood and translated by H. B. Nisbet, Cambridge University Press, 1991, pps. 87-88
42 Ibid. p. 282
43 Ibid. p. 275
44 Ibid. p. 240
45 Hegel, Lectures on the History of Philosophy, translated by E. S. Haldane, Kegan, Paul, Trench, Truebner and Co. London, 1892. Vol 3, p. 54.
46 Hegel, Lectures on the Philosophy of Religion, together with a Work on the Proofs of the Existence of God edited and translated by E. B. Speirs and J. Burdon Sanderson, Kegan, Paul, Trench, Truebner and Co. London, 1895, reprinted by Routledge & Kegan Paul, London, p. 303.
47 Hegel, Phenomenology of Spirit, translated by A. V. Miller, Oxford University Press, Oxford, 1977, p. 11.
48 Hegel, The Philosophy of History, New York, 1956, translated by J. Sibree, p. 36.
49 Reading Hegel: The Introductions edited by Aakash Singh and Rimina Mohapatra, re.press, Melbourne, Australia, 2008, pps. 128 and 126.
50 Ibid.
51 Hegel, The Letters, translated by Clark Butler and Christiane Seiler, Indiana University Press, 1984, p. 114
52 Reading Hegel: The Introductions edited by Aakash Singh and Rimina Mohapatra, re.press, Melbourne, Australia, 2008, p. 129.
53 Hegel, Introduction to the Philosophy of History, translated by Leo Rauch, Hackett, Indianapolis, 1988, p. 12.
54 Georg Wilhelm Friedrich Hegel, Elements of the Philosophy of Right, edited by Allen W. Wood and translated by H. B. Nisbet, Cambridge University Press, 1991, p. 20.
55 Ibid. p. 312.
56 Reading Hegel: The Introductions edited by Aakash Singh and Rimina Mohapatra, re.press, Melbourne, Australia, 2008, p. 126.
57 Hegel, Phenomenology of Spirit, translated by A. V. Miller, Oxford University Press, Oxford, 1977, p. 51.
58 Ibid. p. 485.

59 Ibid. p. 492.
60 Ibid. p. 110.
61 Ibid. p. 492.
62 Ibid. p. 33.
63 Ibid. p. 458.
64 Georg Wilhelm Friedrich Hegel, Elements of the Philosophy of Right, edited by Allen W. Wood and translated by H. B. Nisbet, Cambridge University Press, 1991, p. 279.
65 Hegel, The Philosophy of History, New York, 1956, translated by J. Sibree, p. 234
66 Hegel, Phenomenology of Spirit, translated by A. V. Miller, Oxford University Press, Oxford, 1977, p. 5.
67 Ibid.
68 Ibid. p. 3
69 Ibid. p. 493.
70 Reading Hegel: The Introductions edited by Aakash Singh and Rimina Mohapatra, re.press, Melbourne, Australia, 2008, p. 117.
71 Hegel, Phenomenology of Spirit, translated by A. V. Miller, Oxford University Press, Oxford, 1977, p. 44.
72 Reading Hegel: The Introductions edited by Aakash Singh and Rimina Mohapatra, re.press, Melbourne, Australia, 2008, p. 128.
73 Hegel, Phenomenology of Spirit, translated by A. V. Miller, Oxford University Press, Oxford, 1977, p. 28.
74 Ibid. p. 19.
75 Ibid.
76 Ibid.
77 Hegel, Introduction to Lectures on the Philosophy of History, in: Reading Hegel: The Introductions edited by Aakash Singh and Rimina Mohapatra, re.press, Melbourne, Australia, 2008, p. 122.
78 Bertolt Brecht, Die Gedichte, Suhrkamp, Frankfurt-am-Main, 2000, p. 182.
79 Hegel, Phenomenology of Spirit, translated by A. V. Miller, Oxford University Press, Oxford, 1977, p. 18.

Already published in the same series:

Walther Ziegler
Camus in 60 Minutes
ISBN 9783741227738

Walther Ziegler
Freud in 60 Minutes
ISBN 9783741227707

Walther Ziegler
Hegel in 60 Minutes
ISBN 9783741227677

Walther Ziegler
Heidegger in 60 Minutes
ISBN 9783741227752

Walther Ziegler
Kant in 60 Minutes
ISBN 9783741226373

Walther Ziegler
Marx in 60 Minutes
ISBN 9783741227691

Walther Ziegler
Platon in 60 Minutes
ISBN 9783741227615

Walther Ziegler
Rousseau in 60 Minutes
ISBN 9783741227622

Walther Ziegler
Sartre in 60 Minutes
ISBN 9783741227653

Walther Ziegler
Smith in 60 Minutes
ISBN 9783741227721

Coming soon in the same series:

Walther Ziegler
Adorno in 60 Minutes

Walther Ziegler
Arendt in 60 Minutes

Walther Ziegler
Bacon in 60 Minutes

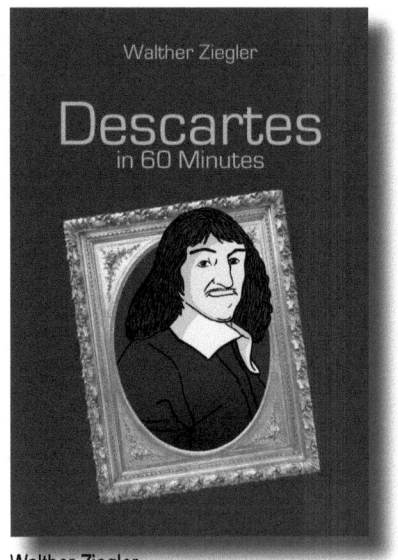

Walther Ziegler
Descartes in 60 Minutes

Walther Ziegler
Foucault in 60 Minutes

Walther Ziegler
Habermas in 60 Minutes

Walther Ziegler
Hobbes in 60 Minutes

Walther Ziegler
Nietzsche in 60 Minutes

Walther Ziegler
Popper in 60 Minutes

Walther Ziegler
Rawls in 60 Minutes

Walther Ziegler
Schopenhauer in 60 Minutes

Walther Ziegler
Wittgenstein in 60 Minutes

The author:

Dr Walther Ziegler is academically trained in the fields of philosophy, history and political science. As a foreign correspondent, reporter and newsroom coordinator for the German TV station ProSieben he has produced films on every continent. His news reports have won several prizes and awards. He has also authored numerous books in the field of philosophy. His many years of experience as a journalist mean that he is able to present the complex ideas of the great philosophers in a way that is both engaging and very clear. Since 2007 he has also been active as a teacher and trainer of young TV journalists in Munich, holding the post of Academic Director at the Media Academy, an institute of higher education that offers film and TV courses at its base directly on the site of the major European film production company Bavaria Film.